P9-CAM-775

My
Id-al-Fitr

Monica Hughes

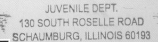

Raintree

Chicago, Illinois

3 1257 01708 2594

© 2004 Raintree
Published by Raintree, a division of Reed Elsevier, Inc.
Chicago, Illinois
Customer Service 888-363-4266
Visit our website at www.raintreelibrary.com

For information, address the publisher:
Raintree, 100 N. LaSalle, Suite 1200, Chicago, IL 60602

Printed and bound in the United States at Lake Book Manufacturing, Inc.
07 06 05 04 03
10 9 8 7 6 5 4 3 2 1

Library of Congress Cataloging-in-Publication Data:
Hughes, Monica.
  My Id-al-Fitr / Monica Hughes.
    p. cm. -- (Festivals)
Summary: Illustrations and simple text describe how one family
celebrates Id-al-Fitr.
Includes bibliographical references and index.
  ISBN 1-4109-0640-X (library binding) -- ISBN 1-4109-0666-3 (pbk.)
  1. °åId al-Fiòtr--Juvenile literature. 2. Islam--Customs and
practices--Juvenile literature. [1. °åId al-Fiòtr. 2. Fasts and
feasts--Islam. 3. Islam--Customs and practices. 4. Holidays.] I.
Title. II. Series: Hughes, Monica.   Festivals.
  BP186.45.H84 2003
  297.3'6--dc21
                          2003010855

Acknowledgments
The Publishers would like to thank p. 15 Chris Schwarz and Trip/H. Rogers and p. 22 Peter Sanders for permission
to reproduce photographs.

Cover photograph of the children opening presents, reproduced with permission of Chris Schwarz

Every effort has been made to contact copyright holders of any material reproduced in this book.
Any omissions will be rectified in subsequent printings if notice is given to the publishers.

Some words are shown in bold, **like this.** You can find out
what they mean by looking in the glossary on page 24.

Contents

Getting Ready for Id 4

Id-al-Fitr at School 6

Ramadan 8

Koran School 10

New Moon 12

New Clothes 14

Id Fun 16

Going to the Mosque 18

Family and Friends 20

Id Presents 22

Glossary 24

Index 24

Getting Ready for Id

Id-al-Fitr is a **Muslim** holiday.
We send Id cards to our
family and friends.

I help Mom make special foods for Id.

Id-al-Fitr at School

We talk about **Id-al-Fitr** at school. Our class is making cards for Id.

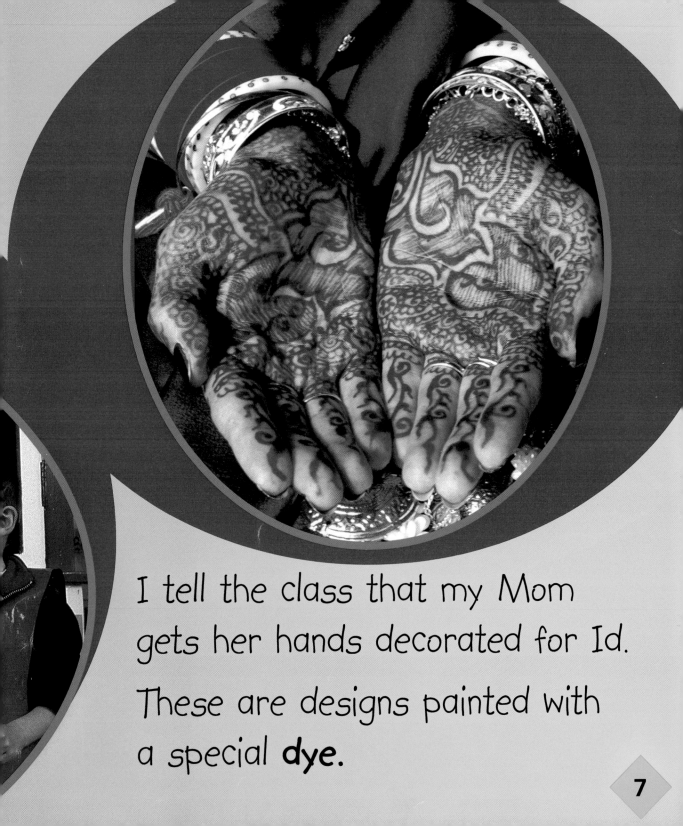

I tell the class that my Mom
gets her hands decorated for Id.
These are designs painted with
a special **dye.**

Koran School

The **Koran** is the **Muslim holy** book.
We study it at Koran school.

Koran school is at the **mosque**.
We learn to say our prayers there.

Ramadan

During **Ramadan**, we **fast** during the day.

At night, we eat **dates**.

We say our prayers at home.

We wait for **Id-al-Fitr.**

New Moon

Ramadan ends when someone sees the new moon.

My family listens to the radio.

New Clothes

Everyone gets new clothes for **Id**.

We wear our new clothes.

15

Dad is buying my brother some special sweets.

17

Going to the Mosque

Now it is **Id-al-Fitr** night. My family goes to the **mosque.**

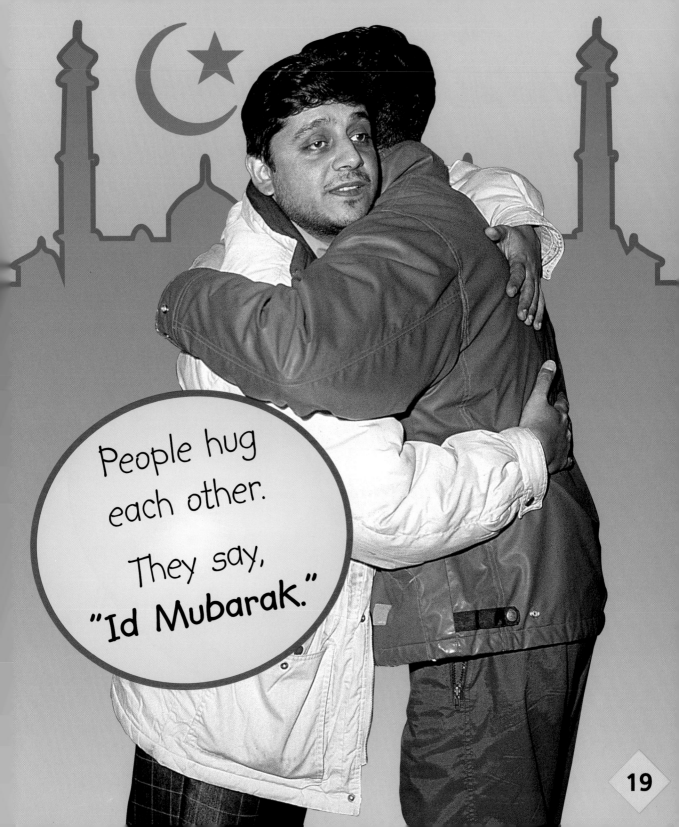

People hug each other.

They say, "Id Mubarak."

Family and Friends

We share a special meal
with our family and friends.

We have an **Id** party.

21

Id Presents

We give each other presents at **Id**.
We also give money to help
other people.

Glossary

bangles   round bracelets

dates   sweet fruit that grows on palm trees

dye   color that can be put on hair, skin, and clothes

fast   to eat and drink very little

holy   something very important and special having to do with God

Id-al-Fitr (You say EED-al-Feetr.) most important Muslim holiday that comes at the end of the month of Ramadan, and is a time when people celebrate by giving money and food to the poor. Id-al-Fitr is called Id for short.

Id Mubarak (You say EED muh-BARE-ak) a Muslim greeting that means "Peace to you"

Koran (You say KUH-ran.) the Muslim holy book. It is written in Arabic, a language from the Middle East.

mosque (You say MOS-k.) place where Muslims go to worship God

muslim   religion based on the teachings of a holy man named Mohammed

Ramadan (You say RAHM-uh-don.) a month in the Muslim religion when people fast and pray. Id-al-Fitr is celebrated at the end of Ramadan.

Index

cards. 4, 6

clothes. 14, 15

family. 4, 12, 18, 20

food 5, 10, 17

friends. 4, 20

money 22

moon 12, 13

mosque. 9, 18

party 21

presents 22

Koran school 8, 9